Notebook Not Ebook
Blank Notebook with 120 pages

© 2014 by Spicy Journals

All rights reserved. No part of this publication may be reproduced, stored in a retrieval system or transmitted in any form by any means, electronic, mechanical, photocopying, recording, scanning or otherwise without the permission of Spicy Journals.

For more journals and notebooks visit:
www.spicyjournals.com

CPSIA information can be obtained
at www.ICGtesting.com
Printed in the USA
LVOW04s0306020318
568435LV00001BA/1/P